MARGARET MAHY has published over 200 books and is ack
all over the world as one of the outstanding children's writers of today.
Twice winner of the Carnegie Medal, several of her books
have become modern classics. Her previous books for Frances Lincoln are
Simply ous!, *Dashing Dog* and *Down the Dragon's Tongue*.
In 2006, M ret was awarded the Hans Christian Andersen Medal,
the est interr tional recognition granted to authors
and lustrators of children's books.

DUNBAR was born in Stratford upon Avon.
nter of the children's author Joyce Dunbar,
first started illustrating when she was 16
and has ree in illustration from the University of Brighton.
as named 'Most Promising New Illustrator'
Publisher's Weekly's 2004 Cuffie Awards.
Her ook for Frances Lincoln was *Looking After Louis*.

To those twin rascals Julia and Biddy... I have often tried
to find you down the back of the chair – M.M.

For Lucy Neale, with love – P.D.

Down the Back of the Chair copyright © Frances Lincoln Limited 2006
Text copyright © Margaret Mahy 2006
Illustrations copyright © Polly Dunbar 2006

The right of Margaret Mahy to be identified as the author
and of Polly Dunbar to be identified as the illustrator of this work
has been asserted by them in accordance with the
Copyright, Designs and Patents Act, 1988 (United Kingdom).

First published in Great Britain in 2006 by
Frances Lincoln Children's Books, 4 Torriano Mews,
Torriano Avenue, London NW5 2RZ
www.franceslincoln.com

First paperback edition 2007

British Library Cataloguing in Publication Data
available on request.

ISBN 978-1-84507-602-3

Printed in China

9 8 7 6 5 4 3 2

Down the Back of the Chair

Margaret Mahy

Illustrated by Polly Dunbar

FRANCES

LINCOLN

CHILDREN'S

BOOKS

Our car is slow to start and go.
We can't afford a new one.
Now, if you please, Dad's lost the keys.
We're facing rack and ruin.

No car, no work! No work, no pay!
We're growing poorer day by day.
No wonder Dad is turning grey.
The morning is a blue one.

Nothing but dockets
in his pockets,
raging with despair,

Dad acts appalled!
Though nearly bald,
he tries to tear his hair.

But Mary,
who is barely two,
says, "Dad should do
what I would do!

I lose a lot, but I find a few —
down the back of the chair."

He's patted himself and searched the shelf.
He's hunted here and there,
so now he'll kneel and try to feel
right down the back of the chair.

Oh, it seemed to grin as his hand went in.
He felt tingling under his skin.
What will a troubled father win
from down the back of the chair?

Some hairy string and a diamond ring

were down the back of the chair.

Pine apple peel and a conger eel

were down the back of the chair.

A sip, a sup, a sop, a song, a spider seven inches long.

No wonder that it smells so strong — down the back of the chair.

A packet of pins
and **one of the twins,**
down the back of the chair.

A pan, a fan that belonged to Gran,

down the back of the chair...

A crumb,

a comb,

a clown,

a cap,

a pirate with a treasure map,

a dragon trying to take a nap —

down the back

of the chair.

A cake, a drake, a smiling snake,

down the back of the chair.

A string of pearls,
a lion with curls,
down the back
of the chair.

A skink, a skunk, a skate, a ski,

a couple of elephants

drinking tea,

a bandicoot and a bumblebee, down the back of the chair.

But what is this?

Oh, bliss! Oh, bliss!

Down the back of the chair.

The long lost will

of Uncle Bill,

down the back

of the chair.

His money box all crammed with cash,
tangled up in a scarlet sash.
There's pleasure, treasure, toys and trash –
down the back of the chair.

"I've found my dreams,"

our father beams,

"down the back of the chair.

At last I see

how life can be,

down the back

of the chair."

"Forget the keys! We're poor no more.
Just call a taxi to the door."

A taxi shot out with a roar

from down the back of the chair.

The chair
the chair,
the challenging chair,
the champion chair, the cheerful chair,
the charming chair, the children's chair,
the chopped and chipped, but chosen chair.
To think our fortune
waited there -
down the back
of the
chair!

MORE STORIES BY MARGARET MAHY
FROM FRANCES LINCOLN CHILDREN'S BOOKS

DASHING DOG
Illustrated by Sarah Garland

Follow the chaotic antics of the dashing dog and his family
in a mad, dizzy and joyful walk along the beach.
With Margaret Mahy's wildly funny sense of humour
and Sarah Garland's exuberant illustrations, this is a picture book made in heaven!
ISBN 978-0-7112-1977-9

DOWN THE DRAGON'S TONGUE
Illustrated by Patricia MacCarthy

Could anything be more exciting than sliding down a great, big
slippery slide like a dragon's tongue?
Harry and Miranda can't wait to climb up, up, up
to the top of the slide, but Mr Prospero, their father, isn't so sure.
ISBN 978-0-7112-1617-4

SIMPLY DELICIOUS!
Illustrated by Jonathan Allen

Who can resist Mr Minky's double-dip-chocolate-chip-and-cherry ice cream
with rainbow twinkles and chopped-nut sprinkles?
Certainly not toucan, spider monkey, tiger or crocodile.
Can Mr Minky outwit all the wily predators and get home
before the ice cream melts? Just watch him!
ISBN 978-0-7112-1441-5

Frances Lincoln titles are available from all good bookshops.
You can also buy books and find out more about your favourite titles,
authors and illustrators on our website: www.franceslincoln.com